Anonymous

The Lead Pencil Manufactory of A.W. Faber at Stein near Nürnberg, Bavaria

An historical sketch

Anonymous

The Lead Pencil Manufactory of A.W. Faber at Stein near Nürnberg, Bavaria
An historical sketch

ISBN/EAN: 9783337411626

Printed in Europe, USA, Canada, Australia, Japan

Cover: Foto ©ninafisch / pixelio.de

More available books at **www.hansebooks.com**

THE

LEAD PENCIL MANUFACTORY

OF

A. W. FABER

AT

STEIN NEAR NÜRNBERG.

BAVARIA.

An historical sketch,

in commemoration of the Jubilee celebrated in the year 1861 to
mark the completion of the first Century of the existence of the
Establishment, dedicated by the Proprietor to his Patrons and
Business friends.

Nürnberg. Printed by U. E. Sebald.

The lead pencil, as everyone knows, is an invention of modern times, and may unhesitatingly be placed side by side with the numerous improvements and inventions, by means of which the last three centuries in particular have so largely contributed towards the spread of Arts and Sciences and the facilitation of Study and Communication. To the classic ages and their art the pencil and in general every application of lead as a writing material was entirely unknown and it was first in the middle ages, as we hear, that lead was employed for this purpose. This metal however was by no means the same sort of thing as the black lead of our pencils, which are indeed only mentioned in conjunction of lead on account of the writing produced by them bearing some resemblance to lead. Besides which lead was then only used for ruling lines and in no instance for writing or drawing purposes. This leadruler was in form a sharpedged disc, such as is said to have been used for the same purpose even in the later periods of the classic ages.

With the developement and growth of modern painting the traces of pencil-like drawings first begin to manifest themselves. The masters of the fourteenth century, especially van Eyck, and of the fifteenth, such as Memlink and others, appear to be the first who mention works of art executed with a pencil-like instrument upon chalked paper. They are generally designated as drawings in silver-style, this specification however not being capable of any closer confirmation, though this much is certain that the use of pure silver is not intended to be implied. In like manner it is reported of the Italian artists of the latter part of the middle ages, that they drew with a silver-style upon smooth deal covered with the dust of calcined bones, which process appears however only to have met with very partial success.

On the other hand in Italy in the fourteenth century much drawing was done with styles composed of a mixture of lead and tin; drawings that could be effaced with bread crumb.

Petrarch's Laura was delineated by a contemporary in this manner and in the time of Michael Angelo the process was still in use. These styles were then introduced into Germany from Italy, under what particular name, we know not. In Italy they are called "Stile", but even they never seem at any time to have been the universally acknowledged drawing material.

About the same period the pen came into use as a drawing- as well as writing-material, to which were added, in the most flourishing days of painting, black chalk and red chalk which enjoyed extensive use. The Italians obtained the best red chalk from Germany and the best black chalk from Spain. Vasari, speaking of an artist of the sixteenth century, especially remarks that he understood how to use style, pen, black chalk and red chalk with equal dexterity.

To this period belongs also the discovery of black lead and with it the production of an entirely new writing- and drawing-material — The Lead Pencil.

This invention, which conferred so many benefits not only upon practical life but also upon art, was made in England in the reign of Queen Elisabeth, for in the year 1564 the celebrated blacklead mines of Borrowdale in Cumberland were discovered. With the opening of this mine every element was present to render the developement of an extensive pencil trade upon English soil possible.

In the year 1565 the first lead pencils were manufactured in England. The mines of Borrowdale, at one time on account of the valuable nature of their produce exposed even to the predatory attacks of the inhabitants of the neighbouring mountains, supply the English down to the present day with the material for the best English leadpencils. The manufacturing of the lead obtained was simple, the material, as soon as it came out of the mine, being cut to the proper size with a saw and then without any further manipulation fastened into the wood and it is remarkable, that the first pencils made in this manner are acknowledged to be decidedly the best and down to the present day unsurpassed by any other manufacture in the softness and delicacy of the lead. Although the Cumberland pencils were soon in great request as being the first to really meet an exigency long felt, it is their excellent quality that has given them their lasting and universal reputation especially in the World of Art.

The Cumberland mine only remained open for six weeks in the year and yet the blacklead obtained in this short time is stated to have been of the value of £ 40,000 or One Million Francs each time.

The raw material was sent up to London just as it came from the mine and there sold by auction in the b l a c k l e a d m a r k e t, these sales taking place on the first Monday in every month. The price averaged 36 — 40 shillings per English pound and the value of the good Cumberland black lead according to Dufrénoy was 400 Francs per Kilogramme.

The fact of the English Government having considered it expedient rigorously to prohibit the export of black lead in any other form than that of leadpencils goes to prove of what importance these mines and the manufacture of leadpencils in connexion with them was to England. In spite of the fact however that the mines only remained open for six weeks in the year and that no blacklead might be exported from them, the working of the mines, continued as it was for upwards of a century, at last began to have the effect of diminishing the yield, until at last nothing was to be obtained from them but an inferior and impure material no longer adapted as before for the manufacture of pencils.

In order to protect themselves from the consequences of a failure of the Cumberland blacklead mines, the English strenuously sought in every direction for new blacklead deposits, but down to the present day without the desired success. There remained therefore nothing but to look about for some means whereby the impure refuse still obtainable could be purified.

The process invented for this purpose consisted of first grinding the blacklead to powder as soon as it came out of the mine, then purifying it as much as possible from foreign substances by chemical means and finally compressing it by means of a press in such a manner that the mass could be just as easily cut as the pure Cumberland blacklead used to be. However notwithstanding all the appliances of art and science were brought to bear upon the subject and spite of every exertion to render this composition perfect, the English have not hitherto succeeded in producing any material capable of replacing the natural blacklead as obtained from the Cumberland mines.

These circumstances operated as an inducement to search for a substitute, which would admit of a greater economy in the use of blacklead. Experiments were made in England with this view and various substances such as glue, isinglass, tragacanth, gum &c. were tried for the purpose of cementing and consolidating the earthy blacklead into a firm mass. But none of these means succeeded. Subsequently it was attempted to improve the blacklead by melting it with minerals, compounding it with 30 or 40 per cent of sulphur. But this made the blacklead too brittle and the pencils made by this process would hardly mark at all. At last mixing with antimony was tried, which certainly yielded a composition in outward appearance very similar to the pure blacklead, but which proved to be but an unsatisfactory writingmaterial.

Towards the end of last century the manufacture of leadpencils was introduced into France and soon attained to an extensive developement. Hardly were the last restrictions upon industrial freedom removed in that country, when in the year 1795 the idea was started of making use of clay for the purpose of binding the blacklead together. This process soon found favor on account of its many advantages for by this commixture a great portion of the costly blacklead was saved and at the same time the manufacture rendered materially easier, so that the leadpencils could be supplied at a very much cheaper rate.

By these novel improvements a fresh era in the manufacture of leadpencils was commenced in France. Notwithstanding this however, there was yet very much to be done in the department of blackleadpencil manufacture in order to keep pace with the increased requirements of advancing art and more civilised life.

True, various degrees of hardness and different sorts of pencils were thus obtained but these were by no means proportional to the various modes of use. The manipulation of the brittle material demanded deep study, and conscientious laborers in order to give the pencil the requisite perfection.

If we now turn to Germany, it will in the first place be necessary to cast a glance at the developement of German industry and German leadpencil manufacture, it being then shown under what circumstances it had to develope itself and with what rivals it had to enter into competition.

It is not to be denied that from the very first German industry found itself in a more disadvantageous position. France and England had already become intrinsically industrious countries. They possessed immense facilities for foreign trade, the greatest internal freedom of motion for the industrial element, a legislature which took cognizance of all the requirements of industry, in short both countries were, in comparison with Germany, favored by certain circumstances which are indispensably necessary to render industry flourishing and which were then already fulfilled, whereas in Germany political division and animosity and the pressure of the guilds operated most perniciously upon industrial enterprise.

For these reasons industry could only develope itself in Germany later and then but slowly. The transition from the old to the new state of things appeared much more difficult, as many long since antiquated forms, which had become endeared to us by use, had first to be abolished.

The Saxon spirit, which, on the other side of the Channel had attained to such glorious results, had to sustain many a conflict in its native land, and many a praiseworthy attempt suffered shipwreck on the many obstacles, which the splitting up of the nation and the retention of unfeasable arrangements opposed to every great idea.

German science flourished at the same time to a very great extent, but in its exaltation it stood too high above ordinary life, not perceiving how to associate itself with it, so as to penetrate it with its enlightening and warmthgiving rays. Thus German industry remained far behind foreign enterprise and Germany beheld herself inundated with quantities of foreign manufactures, which she herself could have produced just as well, indeed it came to such a pass that foreigners relying upon their well organised commerce and the celebrity of their products even ventured to send German manufactures into the German market, stamped with a foreign trademark.

German industry being at this low ebb, the manufacture of leadpencils occupied but a very modest place. The first traces are to be found in the village of Stein not far from Nürnberg. As far back as the year 1726 the churchbooks mention marriages of „Pencilmakers", subsequently also „Black-lead cutters" male and female.

Leadpencil making however was then in its very lowest state, as in no case is a large establishment mentioned, and it may be assumed that this branch of trade was only just able to maintain a precarious position in comparison with the English manufacture.

The Bavarian government however soon devoted their attention to this branch of industry and sought to advance it. In the year 1766 a Count von Kronsfeld received a concession for the erection of a leadpencil manufactory at Jettenbach.

But the manufacture, wanting as it was in material, experience and custom, still remained so insignificant, that in "Beckmanns Technologie", which appeared in the year 1777 "Pencilmaking" merely received a quite superficial and incidental notice.

In the year 1816 the Bavarian government erected a Royal Leadpencil manufactory at Obernzell (Hafnerzell) and introduced into this establishment the French process already mentioned of using clay to consolidate the blacklead.

When the new manufacture was in full play, the government transferred the whole establishment into private hands as was intended from the commencement, though the credit of having given the impetus to renewed activity on a large scale certainly belongs to it.

The establishment is now in the possession of the renowned Regensburg manufacturer. In addition to this the leadpencil manufacture had taken root in Vienna and an establishment was formed there, in which likewise the French process of mixing the blacklead with clay was adopted.

The now so extensive lead pencil manufactory at Stein sprung from very modest beginnings. In the year 1760 namely its founder, **Kaspar Faber,** settled in this village of Stein three miles from Nürnberg, and in the year 1761 commenced the manufacture of leadpencils.

At that time adverse external circumstances pressed heavily upon the young manufactory, the whole possessions of its founder consisting only of a small house situated on the Rednitz and surrounded by a small garden. A judicial inventory dated 1786 still preserved in the family specifies faithfully the insignificant property possessed by them, showing a nett result of „Fifty nine florins".

The finest and dearest qualities mentioned therein are spoken of as „several gross of English pencils", for thus the better German manufactures had to disguise themselves under a foreign title. The demand for these manufactures was trifling and purely local, as the spirit of commerce and enterprise did but little to assist their introduction.

Nürnberg and Fürth appear to have been the first to patronise the products of the manufactory. To these places, as we know, the pencils finished in the course of the week were carried on Saturdays in a basket; but the fact of their having been well paid for goes to prove that even then their excellence was acknowledged. The relations at that time existing between the producer and the consuming public were however but little regulated. The producer stood by himself alone, cut off from the world, which seemed to him too immensely large for him to dare to step out into it. The farsighted vision, searching in every direction to discover new wants and invent new improvements, were wanting to him, as was also the beneficial influence of external relations, with which he was never brought in contact.

Nor was the consumer any more favorably situated.

The article became the object of extensive commercial speculation and had often to travel a very long way before it reached the hands of the consuming public, nor was the repute of a good name any guarantee to the consumer of the excellence of the article, for in order to keep the manufacturers in complete dependance, the merchants would not allow them to mark their better products with their names, but prescribed them foreign names and unmeaning signs, such as: Harps, Stars etc.

It was but slowly that the French process of mixing the lead with clay gained ground and many years after the adoption of this process the workmen, even in Faber's manufactory, were still employed in working the Spanish lead in the old fashioned way by melting it and cutting it with a saw.

The progress of the French however soon forced the merchants to press the Nürnberg manufacturers to advance, so as not to be left behind by competition. After the introduction of the new composition the Nürnberg manufactories soon found themselves favorably circumstanced and yielded satisfactory profits both to the merchants and the manufacturers.

But this was not to last. In the first ten years of this century competition increased steadily and enormously so that demand by no means kept pace with supply, and the vital question forced itself upon the manufacturers, whether they were in a position to produce the article either better or cheaper?

This difficult problem was however solved in a manner unfavorable to the manufacture, and with that revolution commences the decay of the same which now began to make itself felt.

The manufacture had, as before observed, become dependant upon the trade of Nürnberg, which however no longer occupied its former high position, for, although a considerable trade with foreign lands still existed, it was to a great extent nominal. The enlargement and correction of ideas by foreign travel and personal acquaintance with the grand advancement in foreign industry, were wanting and thus no beneficial adjustment of the Nürnberg manufacture could be brought about. Manufacture became the shuttlecock of commercial speculation, which could not even so much as claim the credit of having successfully met the increased requirements of the age or put a stop to powerful competition or an overworked system of trade more calculated for the future.

The trade of Nürnberg at that time lay in the fetters of the guild system, the relic of an earlier golden time, which, aiming at the isolation of industry, which was thereby given into its hands, was the ban that opposed its progress for a length of time, alluring it to act contrary to the interests of native industry and therefore contrary to its own interests.

How much did this system leave of the ancient splendor and well earnt renown of the City of Nürnberg? — A minimum kept and retained solely and alone by the self denial, frugality and industry of the inhabitants. The ingenious, serviceable articles had disappeared, giving place to goods, whose only recommendation consisted in their being unprecedentedly cheap. The endeavour to manufacture without the least regard to quality or serviceability as long as cheapness was attained had become a rooted evil increasing as it descended in all its fulness from father to son. The honorable distinction of the title „Nuernberg, good" soon became changed into the lasting and contemptuous one of „Nürnberg goods" and in the business world people even went so far as to say that nothing good could possibly be produced at Nürnberg.

These circumstances, which are to be laid to the account not only of individuals but likewise of a domineering system and the spirit of a time not so very far distant even now, attest that real industrial activity must go hand in hand with mercantile spirit in order to maintain itself in the world free from the influences above pointed out and enter the lists with competition. It is only emancipated industry that can congratulate itself on real progress and improve the article only by having an eye to the requirements of the consumer.

It was under these circumstances that **Anton Wilhelm Faber,** the son of the founder, whose name the firm still bears, and since 1810 **Georg Leonhard Faber,** the father of the present proprietor, stood at the head of the establishment.

Many improvements had been attempted and several adopted; much valuable experience had been gained, many processes in the manufacture had been perfected and a number of intelligent workmen drawn together; spite of all this however the mercantile relations above described operated most perniciously upon the manufactory.

The mode of manufacture induced by the enslavement of industry on the part of trade more especially destroyed that conscientious strictness, which must form the foundation of a solid industry. Things went so far that articles were sent forth into the world, possessing the outward appearance of pencils, the wood being just tipped with lead at each end as though it was properly filled, whereas in fact you only had a useless stick of wood before you.

Such swindling impositions, sent forth by the Nürnberg manufactories into foreign countries, were well calculated to bring about a complete collapse and it is difficult to regain confidence once deceived or esteem once forfeited. But it must not be supposed that the interests of the Nürnberg pencil manufacture were not solid. The unscrupulous transactions on part of some establishments as a matter of course damaged the reputation of those which carried on their business in an industrious and conscientious manner and the renown of the whole trade was thus placed in jeopardy.

In the year 1839 the present proprietor **Johann Lothar Faber** undertook the management of the manufactory upon the death of his father Georg Leonhard Faber abovenamed.

This gentleman had, down to his nineteenth year, endeavoured as far as possible to perfect his commercial education in Nuernberg in the most fundamental and general manner and, from his earliest youth, especially devoted himself to the study of everything at all bearing upon his father's manufactory. Even at that time he directed his attention not merely to his father's affairs, but also to the developement of a business so sadly crippled and underwent many privations in order as much as possible to satisfy the manifold claims laid upon him by the aim which was always present to his imagination.

When nineteen years of age he went to Paris in order to increase his stock of knowledge. There, in that capital of the World a greater range of vision was opened to him and he beheld the operation of that restless spirit of enterprise, which so mightily stirs the heart of the country. For the first time the youth was brought face to face with the enormous business carried on both with France and foreign lands and of which Paris is the centre. He surveyed the fruits of a free, active industry, the great highroads, upon which commerce flows from the mother country to distant lands, the realisation of a colossal traffic, which allows no article to escape its observation and flows in an ever moving wave between purchasers and consumers. Then his thoughts were carried back to his distant native land with its industry so cramped and fettered as to be altogether estranged from the great markets of the world and the possibility flashed across his mind, that matters might be rendered very different at home and native industry not only reconquer its honour and the renown of its pristine good name, but that it might also be led forth from its narrow prison and enabled to compete with the vigour and intelligence of the markets of the world and that it would thus ensure obtaining an honourable position.

At that time industrial life was in full activity at Paris, scarcely

six years having elapsed since the revolution of July and Louis Philippe being
firmly established on the constitutional citizen-throne.

Thus great hopes filled the breast of the young man and impelled him
to follow up the ideas and plans of life he had adopted with all his energy.

After a sojourn of three years in Paris there fell upon him suddenly
and unexpectedly, on the midst of his labours, the news of the death of his
father and after first performing a previously contemplated journey to London,
in order to enrich his store of knowledge and experience, he returned to his
native land in August 1839.

Now was the time to carry out and realise all the ideas he had imbibed.
The condition of his father's manufactory was, as before stated, extremely unsatisfactory. Scarcely twenty workmen were employed and the annual business done
amounted only to about 12000 florins. If that glorious future, which the young
man had assigned to the manufactory in his imagination at Paris was to become
a fact, it would involve carrying on a conflict with all the old perverted notions,
to break with the cumbersome progress of former times and upon the ruins of
the Nürnberg trade, which beheld itself excluded from the world's market, to
lay the foundations of a new commerce, which alone would be able to reconquer
for the venerable commercial city of Nürnberg her ancient renown.

He was the man, who brought, in the first place certainly only the
pencil manufacture, but therewith also native industry in general, into direct
contact with the ideas of foreign countries.

Sure and gradual progress was however indispensable. The new proprietor adopted the device of:

„Truth, Respectability, Industry"

as the fundamental principle of his dealings, being firmly convinced, that no human
undertaking, which aspires to a future and lasting success, can possibly exist,
if it in any respect be based upon untruth, or at variance with that, which
passes for right and respectable among men in general or, which ignores the
duty of unwearying activity and energetic industry. These principles seemed to

him all the more indispensable for his manufactory as he, by his position, rendered himself to a certain extent responsible for the weal and woe of so many souls.

The two brothers of the new proprietor had been destined by their father for other modes of occupation, there being at that time no prospect of the pencil manufacture maintaining them.

The present proprietor of the manufactory however, feeling confident of the success of his comprehensive schemes, took to himself in the year 1840 his second youngest brother **Johann Faber,** who at that time carried on an Hotel at Prague, in order to unite his activity with his own.

The pencils were then only manufactured in proportionally few and cheap sorts, but the new proprietor of the manufactory was soon induced to introduce finer sorts at proportionate prices.

While still at Paris he had endeavoured in every way by letters to his father to conduce towards the elevation of the manufactory and the improvement of the quality of the articles manufactured, but it was when he began to put his hands to the work himself that he first aimed at any material success.

These improved manufactures and especially his new so called Polygrade Pencils, which have met with the greatest renown especially among artists, were all marked with the name of the firm and, as they by reason of their increased price, the unavoidable consequence of improved quality, met with but little countenance among the Nürnberg merchants, the manufacturer travelled with them himself through Germany, Russia, Austria, Belgium, Holland, France, England, Italy and Switzerland and opened up business connexions with all the chief cities of Europe, which, with the continued improvements in his manufactures, soon found him a satisfactory custom and an ever increasing demand, important enough to raise itself above the narrow sphere of local interests.

In the interior of the manufactory too great improvements were undertaken, as nearly every year called for some new addition. In these new erections care was taken to construct them as roomy and light as possible, thus taking into consideration the health of the workmen and the fact that work is much better performed in sunny spacious rooms, than in gloomy dark vaults in which the air cannot be renewed, and that the pleasure and zest with which it is performed redounds to the benefit of the manufactory itself.

The countless departments of business, in which pencils are used, by degrees rendered an extensive and systematic classification necessary from the long easel-pencil to the smallest pocketbook-pencil.

The manufacture had, in consequence of its extensive foreign connexions, already become considerably improved and extended and the varying tastes, even the varying customs of the nations which used them, had to be taken into consideration. The manufacturer never ceased to study all wants, to subject his manufactures constantly to new trials, to avail himself of fresh experiences in order to surpass with his products all similar articles if possible.

The renown of his manufactures has penetrated to all parts of the world and it is not merely their widely extended use, that attests their excellence, but more especially the voice of those men, who make the greatest demands upon the manufactory. There are few Architects and Engineers who use any other article but Faber's pencils, and the whole profession of artists has long since proclaimed A. W. Faber's pencil to be the very best for drawing purposes. Such men as Cornelius, Kaulbach, Bendemann, Lessing, Horace Vernet have expressed themselves to this effect.

In accordance with this verdict is the result of the competition in the several industrial Exhibitions, both at home and abroad, in which Faber's pencils gained the victory over all other manufactures of the same nature.

With the year 1849 a new era in the activity of the manufactory commenced. Ever since that year the products of the manufactory had met with recognition and custom in America and with the continued increase of the population it was to be assumed that the sale of the same would also constantly increase in importance, especially as the manufacture of leadpencils had not as yet taken firm root there and it therefore became a question of obtaining a generally acknowledged product of European manufacture, the excellence of which had been proved by the experience of years and its honest manufacture.

This induced the proprietor of the manufactory to establish a house at New-York and entrust the management of the same to his youngest brother **Eberhard Faber,** who had just completed his study for the law at the universities of Berlin and Erlangen and was at that time engaged in acquiring the necessary mercantile knowledge in the establishment at Stein.

The trade with America thereby acquired a firm footing, the communication spite of the great distance became more regular and the connexion of the manufactory with the new world more close. As England, France, Russia, Italy and the East had long since been open to Faber's manufactures, the idea of creating an universal trade appeared to be realised.

As in the American commercial metropolis, so also in Paris a house was founded, not merely to manage the important trade with France and the neighbouring countries, but also to minister to the fine tastes and elegant requirements of the French, which are of so much advantage to any product intrinsically excellent.

In like manner, in order to supply the requirements of England, India and Australia, an agency was established in London in the year 1851 with Mr A. Heintzmann, now Heintzmann & Rochussen, of N° 9 Friday Street, City, E. C.

While thus the external relations of the manufactory continued steadily to extend themselves, its internal developement likewise advanced step by step.

On the very spot, where once the little house stood, the extensive factory premises are now erected on either side of the Rednitz, the water power of which river proving too insufficient and fluctuating, steam had to be called into requisition and a large engine erected.

As already stated, almost each year demanded an addition to the premises and considerable enlargements and alterations rendered necessary partly by the constantly increasing business and partly by sanatory or ornamental considerations, so that the very character of the locality underwent considerable change.

Gardens now enclose the whole establishment on three of its sides. In one of them stands the residence of the proprietor of the manufactory, Lothar, visible from afar by reason of the height of its situation and remarkable on account of the peculiarity of the style of its architecture; in the other the house of his younger brother, Johann, so that everything stands together in the closest connexion like the life of a large family.

The proprietor, while endeavouring in every way to advance all the ends of the manufactory in the most perfect manner, has not omitted to bear in mind at the same time the moral and material welfare of his workmen, whom he has accustomed himself to recognise as men and his fellow creatures.

In their interest there were in the first place factory rules drawn up, which regulated the duties and rights of the individual in the most precise manner and especially took cognisance of the moral conduct of the workman. They also gave the most diligent workmen and such as were more advanced in years, opportunities of increasing their income by ensuring them an increase of pay under certain conditions.

In order to awaken and encourage a spirit of frugality in the men and to render their future more comfortable and independant, a Workman's Savings Bank was instituted, with the following fundamental principles: Acceptance of the smallest deposit at any time; interest at four per cent to commence as soon as the deposit reaches the amount of five florins; deposits to be withdrawn only on account of some notoriously pressing necessity. This institution found immediate recognition and by degrees came into almost general favor, so that now many an individual, who formerly had to battle with economical cares, finds himself in the possession of a little property and rejoices in his wellregulated family affairs.

There is likewise a special fund for sickness.

A library has also been founded by the master of the manufactory, accessible both to the workman and his family and well used by them, at the same time too an infant school was started for the children of the work people. He likewise originated and supported with his own means the erection of a new schoolhouse, and embraced every opportunity of advancing the education therein.

The social life of the workmen was also taken into consideration and the taste for more elevating amusements, invigorating alike to soul and body, encouraged. Of an evening they would meet in two singing societies to indulge in the good German song, or on Sundays they would amuse themselves with the crossbow in the free, fresh air of God's Nature in the neighbouring forest, or again on festive occasions they would all meet together like one large united family for a sociable convivial repast.

Finally, care was also taken that the workman should mix with the world outside the factory, for which purpose a number of them were sent by the master of the factory to the Industrial Exhibition at Munich in order that they might themselves see the fruit of their labour publicly exposed to view and honorably mentioned, and at the same time obtain a glimpse of other branches of industry.

Further, in order to provide new dwellings for the workmen a large building was erected, of pleasing external proportions, and other buildings were converted into workmen's dwellings. The houses themselves contain separate apartments, which afford the families at a low rent a much pleasanter abode than could be obtained in most of the houses in the towns. Nor is there any constraint; the houses are open to any body and the domestic regulations introduced in the interests of the community are of that nature, that they are cheerfully complied with by everyone. Thus there reigns in these premises a spirit of order and contentment, which alone can make life agreeable.

The village of Stein did not formerly possess any church. For years all exertions to found a separate parish there remained fruitless, until at last the year 1861 brought their reward and in that year, in which the manufactory celebrated its hundredth anniversary, the peaceful clang of the bells for the first time invited the faithful to divine service in the newly erected church, the cost of which had been defrayed by the master of the factory entirely from his own means, out of concern for the spiritual welfare of his workpeople and attachment to his own native place.

The formerly neglected little village has assumed quite a different appearance since then. From afar the slender gothic steeple of the church may be seen rearing its pinnacle proudly aloft, while the smoke of the surrounding shafts tell of busy industry and labour. The former picture of want has given place to a certain degree of wealth and the little garden of the humble house been converted into two large parks.

Simultaneously however with this prosperity in general the manufactory had of course to experience some unpleasant incidents and obstinate struggles. The universal demand for Faber's manufactures was not slow in inducing other manufacturers to imitate and pirate the trademark of the manufactory, which is to be found on all articles manufactured there, and thus to pass off upon the public spurious goods possessing nothing more than the external similarity to the genuine articles, and which could scarcely aspire to mediocrity, which frauds were often repeated, coming to light in various countries.

The manufacturing firm of Rubenstein at Moscow adopted the plan of making use of Faber's trademark and wrappers for their own manufactures and then to circulate them in the Russian market. These malpractises were carried on for a length of time in spite of every exertion to put a stop to them and the prohibition which the Russian Governement issued against the firm in question. Manufactures with spurious trademarks were constantly turning up in Russia until King Maximilian of Bavaria during his protracted stay at Nürnberg in the year 1855 suppressed the evil. His lively interest for reviving industry had already induced him to decorate the proprietor of the manufactory with the order of merit of St. Michael, firstclass, in the year 1854, on which occasion he likewise honoured the factory at Stein with a visit and made himself acquainted with all the details of its operations from the mouth of the manager of the factory, and as at that time these malpractises were brought before his notice he gave the matter all his attention and promised some assistance.

Nor had we to wait long for this, for shortly afterwards Lothar Faber received a communication from the State ministry of the Royal House and Foreign affairs, stating, that, by the intervention of the Royal Bavarian Embassy at St. Petersburg, the evil had been put a stop to by the Russian Government; all the articles marked with Faber's trademark together with the stamp destroyed, and the manager of the Russian manufactory compelled to give assurance in writing that he would no longer pirate Faber's trademark, in default rendering himself liable to legal penalties.

In New-York similar frauds were also carried on. Pencils manufactured in Nürnberg with Faber's trademark and in precise imitations of his wrappers were imported and sold by the firm of Winterhoff, Piper & C°. Complaint having been made, the Customhouse at New-York, at the instance of the examiner appointed for the department of „Literature, Writingmaterials and fine Arts", detained one case of these spurious articles, whereupon the courts of law prohibited all further sale in the town and county of New-York.

A still more cunning fraud was perpetrated at Nürnberg. A deaf and dumb lithographer by name Georg Wolfgang Faber was put forward, whose name was to be made use of. The similarity of the surname and wrapper exactly copied from those of Faber's manufactory were sufficient to make the public believe that they really had the genuine article from Faber's manufactory before them. On the intervention of the authorities, whom Lothar Faber put in motion, the reputed manufacturer was subjected to an examination, which proved him to be altogether incapable of producing such a thing as a serviceable article and shewed that he had only lent his name to other speculators, whereupon the Royal Government of middle Franconia withdrew the licence for pencil making from the said G. W. Faber.

Proceedings were likewise taken against a Pencilmanufacturer at Fulda, who had manufactured and circulated upwards of seven thousand dozen leadpencils with the false stamp "A. W. Faber". The Criminal Court of the Electorate of Hesse in a decision dated 2nd September 1856, condemned the defendant, on account of fraud, to a pecuniary fine of 50 Thalers and further to four weeks imprisonment, a decision, which the supreme Court of Appeal at Cassel absolutely confirmed. Similar events took place in other countries with like results.

As the proprietor of the factory has hitherto proceeded against many persons at home and abroad who had attempted to manufacture and sell pencils in imitation of those of his firm he will further use all his efforts to suppress every deception foisted upon the public.

In the meanwhile the manufactory assiduously endeavoured to attain to perfection in its products. As the stock of blacklead began to disappear in the mines of Cumberland, it succeeded, by its perfected manipulation of the material, in producing so many grades of hardness and supplying such an extensive variety of pencil, that no demand could present itself without meeting with satisfaction among the great choice of manufactures.

In the opinion of connoisseurs the finest sorts even surpass the best Cumberland leadpencils in their lasting and uniform degrees of hardness, their greater firmness and durability as also in the increased purity of the lead. In addition to this they possess such an amount of softness and delicacy, as to be able to stand comparison in this and every particular with the Cumberland pencils. Besides this, and in addition to several other improvements relating to their external appearance, the most useful and ornamental shapes for pencils of the finer descriptions were devised and introduced, and still more recently the socalled "Artist's pencils" were added to the list of novelties and immediately met with the most universal recognition, which soon stimulated other manufacturers to attempt imitations.

In the midst of these exertions the news was suddenly received, that that, which the English had so long sought for and which the perfected system of manufacture still stood much in need of in order to yield more than was previously possible, had been found. A new blacklead mine had been discovered. Johann Peter Alibert, merchant of the first class at Tabasthus in Siberia, had undertaken an exploring expedition in the mountainous eastern portion of Siberia, partly to search for gold. He examined the sand of the rivers Oka, Belloi, Kitoi and Irkutsk, and in one of the mountain ravines in the vicinity of Irkutsk lighted accidentally upon specimens of pure blacklead. Alibert immediately recognised the value and importance of the material and instituted strict investigations until in the year 1847 after much labor and exertion he arrived at the conviction that, in a branch of the mountain range of Saian among the heights of the Batougol mountains four hundred versts westward of the town of Irkutsk, close to the frontier of China, a primitive deposit of blacklead must exist. He addressed himself at once to the task of opening a mine in order to bring the costly material to the surface.

At first the blacklead met with proved to be no better than the refuse Cumberland blacklead, and upwards of three hundred tons of this quality had to be removed before a deposit of the best and purest blacklead was finally opened up. Pieces were soon obtained weighing as much as eighty pounds. The Academy of Sciences at St. Petersburg, before which body Alibert laid his samples of blacklead for analysis, declared the same to consist of the same elements and possess the same properties and consequently to be of precisely the same nature as the Cumberland blacklead. Alibert now proceeded to England where he visited the declining blacklead mines of Cumberland and convinced himself by personal observation of the exhaustion and decay of the same. He thereupon submitted his samples of blacklead to some of the most extensive English leadpencil manufactories for examination, who unanimously confirmed the verdict of the Academy at St. Petersburg, pronouncing the quality of the Siberian blacklead to be excellent and in no way inferior to the Cumberland lead.

It had cost Alibert eight years of unremitting labour and a capital of one million Francs when he beheld his enterprise crowned with this certainly unexpected success.

He now turned his attention to rendering the newly discovered material available for the manufacture of pencils. Having convinced himself that Faber's manufactory was the most extensive in existence and that it circulated the largest amount of fine goods in the world, he applied to the same with a proposition for an agreement, by virtue of which his blacklead was to be taken solely and exclusively by that establishment for the manufacture of pencils.

The firm on the other hand, having thoroughly convinced themselves that the newly discovered blacklead was quite equal to the genuine and best Cumberland blacklead in quality, willingly entertained this proposition of Alibert's, so that in the year 1856 a contract was entered into between the manufactory and Alibert and sanctioned by the Russian Government, according to which all the blacklead, which comes from the Siberian mines is to be delivered to A. W. Faber's manufactory, and to no other establishment for the purposes of pencil manufacture, now and for all time.

It was a mighty work which the restless energy of Alibert had brought into execution in a land so difficult of access. On the summit of the mountain of Batongol, which now in the Russian maps of the country is designated by the name of „Alibertsberg" in honorable remembrance of the discoverer of the blacklead mine, Alibert assembled all his working force and a little colony soon sprung up, which addressed itself zealously to the new mining operations.

The miners brought the blacklead to the surface in large blocks and the material thus obtained proclaimed at once, by its external purity and a beautiful silvery lustre, its excellent value and composition. The transport was attended with immense difficulties. The blocks of blacklead, carefully packed in wooden cases, had to traverse enormous tracts of country, across which not the least vestige of a road is to be found, upon the backs of reindeer to reach the nearest seaport, whence they were shipped to Europe, while other consignments of the blacklead were forwarded to the manufactory exclusively by land.

It may be conceived that Alibert by this discovery drew even the attention of the Russian Government upon himself and was gratified by the kindest encouragement both on part of the Czar and the Governor of the province of Irkutsk, Count Murawiew Amursky. In the report concerning explorations in Siberia issued by the imperial Academy of Sciences the discoverer is mentioned particularly (page 33) and at the same time Faber's manufactory, the capital of which has facilitated and advanced this enterprise, is honorably spoken of.

The manufactory, thus in possession of so extensive a store of black-lead, the excellence of which both theory and practice place on a level with the Borrowdale lead, has produced pencils made with the Siberian lead ever since the year 1856. It was now no longer a question of attaining to the standard of the Cumberland pencils but rather of surpassing it.

The new material was worked partly in a natural state so as to enable connoisseurs to convince themselves of its excellent quality and partly artificially manufactured, which yielded as a result such a degree of evenness, purity and unchanging hardness as had never before been obtained, not even in the best Cumberland pencils. After the exertions of six years the manufactory is just now intending to enter the World's market with its new productions.

Before we conclude our sketch we must stop to contemplate a bright spot in the internal history of the factory and remember the day on which it celebrated the completion of the hundredth year of its existence with a festival, to which the joyful feelings of a happy and contented population and the not less hearty than general participation therein from far and near, lent a peculiar solemnity.

The festival was celebrated by the proprietor of the manufactory **Johann Lothar Faber** and his brother **Johann Faber** together with their families and in the midst of the assembled factory hands male and female, as also of all masterworkmen employed for the manufactory and a large number of invited guests.

The 16th September 1861 was the day fixed for the occasion, chiefly with the view of rendering the festival all the more impressive by a special celebration of divine service in the new church of the village, which had only been consecrated a fortnight before. Preparations of the most varied character occupied both the masters of the factory and their families for some time previously, in order to render this auspicious and happy event a thoroughly joyous festival for their workpeople and all that participated therein, and the remembrance of it no less pleasing than indelible.

Similar feelings however also actuated the workpeople, who exerted themselves with all their power to add to the splendor of the festival, and manifest their good feelings and gratitude in a touching and unexpected manner.

On the eve of the festive day the workmen in a body brought their master a torchlight procession, which, after passing through the whole of the gaily decorated premises, came to halt in the courtyard of Mr. Faber's house, whereupon the workmen's singing club performed three partsongs composed expressly for the occasion.

A deputation of workmen consisting of men who had been longest in the factory then handed the master, together with an appropriate address made by their senior member, a handsome and tasteful album as a festive present from them, and a parchment roll on which were printed a dedication composed in verse, then the speech which a workman made in the most spirited manner previous to the presentation of the album, further the songs performed and a list of the names of all the workmen and women. This was certainly one of the most affecting moments and even those men, who had become grey in the service of the factory were unable to restrain their tears of emotion and gratitude.

Lothar Faber in his reply dwelt particularly upon how he valued the proofs of love, attachment, gratitude and faithfulness shown to him as being not merely intended for himself alone but likewise for his whole house and more especially for his two brothers standing so faithfully by his side, and how he wished that these sentiments of the workpeople might ever spread among them and be manifested to him and his family for all time.

On the morning of the sixteenth of September all the workmen and women assembled at the house of L. Faber in order to receive the festive present appointed for each person as also a commemoration medal coined expressly for this festival, having on the one side the arms of the family with the legend: „Founder: Kaspar Faber † 1784; Successors: A. W. Faber † 1819; G. L. Faber † 1839; J. L. Faber; and upon the Obverse the legend: „In remembrance of the Century Jubilee of the Leadpencil Manufactory of A. W. Faber at Stein near Nürnberg."

The festive clang of bells now summoned all present to the special divine service, which was destined to form a worthy commencement to the festival and all the factory hands arranged themselves in a stately procession, which, headed by the members of the Faber family, moved towards the church in order there to give vent to the feelings of gratitude in a pious and christian manner. A sermon was preached, the text being taken from the 90th Psalm, verses 16. 17 and at the conclusion of the service all the workpeople male and female assembled at eleven o'clock at the workmen's dwellinghouses in the village of Stein built by L. Faber, from whence they started in a procession, headed by the band of the fourteenth regiment of infantry stationed at Nürnberg, for the park of L. Faber, one portion of which nearest the dwellinghouse had been specially arranged for the festival partly for the entertainment of the numerous guests and partly for various amusements of play and dance, and which, by its elegant decorations and appropriate mottoes, bearing upon the past and present of the Factory, made the most agreeable impression upon every one. Arrived upon the festive grounds the entire body of workpeople about four hundred in number partook of the dinner provided for them, the regimental band performing agreeable music the while. The repast concluded, L. Faber mounted a tribune especially erected for this occasion and ornamented with lifesize busts of the departed ancestors, and in a short speech set before them the chief features of the history of the manufactory, impressing upon them, on the commencement of the second century of its existence, the value of that order and carefulness which are so indispensably necessary for the prosperous career of a large establishment in the requirements of our age, and concluding with a cheer for the existence and welfare of the Factory in which all joined vociferously.

The two youngest boys of the family, Wilhelm the son of L. Faber ten years and Ernst the son of his brother Johann, seven years of age hereupon ascended the steps and while the former greeted his father with a poem in the name of the four surviving brothers and sisters of L. Faber, the latter presented him with a silver goblet also in their name as a souvenir of the festival.

By three o'clock the number of the guests had increased to nearly six hundred. They amused themselves with all sorts of games, to which the drawing of prizes lent an especial charm, and with dancing round the loftly maypole erected on the grass plot, or with wandering through the park, which was entirely thrown open, while the band charmed the ear with its performances. In the midst of this lively scene of rejoicing, which partook of the appearance of a national gathering, the Master of the Factory L. Faber, together with all others present were surprised in the most agreeable manner by the arrival of a gracious autographic missive from His Majesty the King, which read as follows:

„On the 16th inst. you celebrate, as I am given to understand the completion of the first Century of the existence of the manufactory founded by your ancestors and whose well earnt fame both at home and abroad redounds to the honor of Bavarian industry. It has likewise given me special pleasure to observe the care, with which you watch over the moral and temporal affairs of your workpeople. The festival which you are about to keep, affords me an opportunity of offering my best congratulations to you and the establishment conducted by you with so much

success and at the same time of expressing the hope that the manufactory
will be blest with continued prosperity.

With the sincerest good wishes

Hohenschwangau 14. September 1861.

Your affectionate King

Max.

To

Mr. Johann Lothar Faber Manufacturer."

With joyous emotion L. Faber communicated this gracious mark of
honour to all assembled, by reading it aloud from the tribune, concluding with
a triple cheer for His Majesty King Max in which every one joined with the
greatest spirit.

He then gave the health of his two brothers, who so faithfully and
energetically second his exertions, which was received with joyous acclamations
echoing again and again from the vast assembly; then his fellowworkers for the
manufactory outside its pale, as also all his business friends and especially the
artists, who. by patronising his manufactures and appreciating their value for
art had so materially contributed to the extension of his fame. L. Faber
thereupon recited a poem the fundamental idea of which was the motto of the
manufactory:

„Truth, Respectability, Industry.“

This recital served as an introduction to the unveiling of an allegorical
tableau executed by Maar of Nürnberg representing partly the activity of the
Factory, and mercantile enterprise, and partly an appropriate allusion to the
Jubilee festival. Then a short address followed by the presentation of a con-
gratulatory testimonial to L. Faber on part of the authorities of the council of
trade of Nürnberg was made, which elicited a cheer for the same. Then Maar
the artist made a speech upon the history of the lead pencil and its application
to Art, thanking L. Faber in the name of his colleagues for the cheer given
them and concluding with a toast for the establishment.

A small brochure setting forth the contents of the Festival Album before mentioned and containing a capital piece of poetry composed by a relation of the Faber family was then distributed among the guests.

A number of speeches and toasts were now made and given by the workmen themselves, who were fairly carried away by excitement, which one and all breathed a spirit of attachment and gratitude, and of which not a few, spite of their simple character, caused feelings of emotion. Performances of their singing clubs alternated with those of the band until as darkness drew near the illumination of the festive grounds and an extensive portion of the park presented a fresh tableau. Bengal lights illumined several of the more lovely points and a pyrotechnic display brought the festival to a conclusion at nine o'clock, when all the participators departed in the gayest spirits and with hearty wishes for the continued prosperity of the Manufactory.

The foregoing description of the Jubilee festival of A. W. Faber's Pencil manufactory may be appropriately closed with the mention of a transaction which was no less a gratification than an honor to the proprietor of the same:

On the morning of the eighth of October a deputation of the magistracy and representatives of the Commune of Nürnberg, consisting of the two Burgomasters, von Wächter and Seiler and the President of the College of the Commune, Dr. Lindner, proceeded to Stein in order to present Johann Lothar Faber with the diploma of honorary citizenship of the City of Nürnberg, which reads as follows:

„The Magistrate and representatives of the Commune of the Royal Bavarian city of Nürnberg have conferred upon Mr. Johann Lothar Faber, proprietor of the Pencil manufactory at Stein in the Royal Jurisdiction of Nürnberg, in appreciation of the many and important services, which he has rendered to industry in general and the trade of Nürnberg in particular, by an unanimous resolution the honorary citizenship of the city of Nürnberg, and, after obtaining the most gracious consent of His Majesty the King, caused this deed to be drawn up for him. Given under the great seal of the city and the signatures of the two Burgomasters as also that of the President of the College of the Commune.

Nürnberg the 16ᵗʰ September 1861.

von Wächter, I. Burgomaster.

Seiler, II. Burgomaster.

Lindner, President of the Presentatives of the Commune."

The celebration of the hundreth anniversary of the existence of the Factory afforded the proprietor of the same a welcome opportunity of dedicating this memoir to all his honoured business friends and patrons as a token of his gratitude and esteem and at the same time of giving them a pretty perfect sketch of his Factory and a view of its internal arrangement. With this latter object he had the nine views, attached to the end hereof, taken, which represent a faithful sketch of the chief points of the establishment and by means of which it is possible to form a tolerably accurate idea of the Lead pencil Manufacture.

The first plate represents the sluicing process. On the left hand side of the picture the blacklead is seen in its original casks, on the right hand side the clay. These two raw materials are here washed and then passed on in pans to be dried.

The second plate shows the grinding which goes on day and night, the composition of blacklead, clay &c. being ground fine while in a wet state, and then dried in ovens especially adapted for that purpose.

The third plate depicts the preparation of the lead. The workmen to the left in the background are forming a plastic mass of the composition by wetting it with water, which while still wet is passed into the cylinder of the press where it is forced through a copper plate, at the bottom of the cylinder, in the centre of which there is an opening of a peculiar shape. As is seen in the representation the lead thus pressed through the cylinder assumes the shape of a ring and is then carried by the workmen on the right upon boards and lying in a straight position, to a moderately warm place to dry. Before however the lead is completely dry, it is cut into sticks of the proper length for filling the pencils. After the drying comes the annealing in peculiarly constructed ovens. This process takes place in hermetically closed vessels of clay or iron in which the sticks of lead are placed in a horizontal position.

In the fourth plate the method of cutting, sawing and planing the wood is seen. In the foreground to the right lies a balk of Florida Cedar wood. These balks are from 10 to 15 feet in length and 8 to 24 inches in thickness. They are first cut across with an upright saw in pieces of the length of a pencil, which pieces are then cut into sticks by small circular saws as shown on the right hand side of the view, the sticks being thereupon planed smooth by the machine in front. Behind the planing machine the grooving machines are situated by means of which the smoothly planed sticks are cut with fine circular saws into top and bottom pieces, the latter of which are furnished with grooves.

The fifth plate represents the process of glueing the sticks of lead into the wood. At each glueing table there are three workmen, one of whom smears the two pieces of wood with glue, while the second places the lead in the groove and the third, after the two pieces are fixed together, trims the pencils, which are then placed in a press and firmly pressed together by means of screws. The round bundles seen in this view are partly finished pencils and partly tops and bottoms.

At this stage of the manufacture the pencils are all square and are now passed on to the planing shop represented in the sixth plate. There they are cut to the exact length by means of fine circular saws and then planed round or square, oval or even hexagonal or trigonal by the planing machines, which they reach in a square form.

The seventh and eighth plates show those operations which are carried on by females.

In the seventh plate to the right the workwomen are seen engaged in polishing the pencils with colours, and to the left those who by means of a lever press stamp the name of the firm upon them.

At last the polished and stamped pencils arrive at the room, where they are made up into packets as represented in the eighth plate. Here they are fastened up in dozens, covered with tickets and packed either by the dozen or the gross.

The ninth plate represents the dwelling houses and manufacturing Premises. The residence on an elevation to the left is that of the proprietor of the Manufactory, below which is seen that of his brother. The two houses in the middle were dwellinghouses in former times and have been used for years as Countinghouse, Warehouse and Sample-show-room. The workshops lower down on the right stand close to the river Rednitz and the machinery therein is set in motion by waterpower, whereas in the other premises higher up steam is the agent employed.

~~mmmm~~

Schlemmen.

Sluicing the lead.

Druckerei von C. Kröll.... Frankfurt a. M.

Druckerei von C. Kreutner, Frankfurt a. M.

Lichtdruck von C. Kreidel, Frankfurt a. M

Fabrik in Stein bei Nürnberg

www.ingramcontent.com/pod-product-compliance
Lightning Source LLC
Chambersburg PA
CBHW031817090426
42739CB00008B/1312